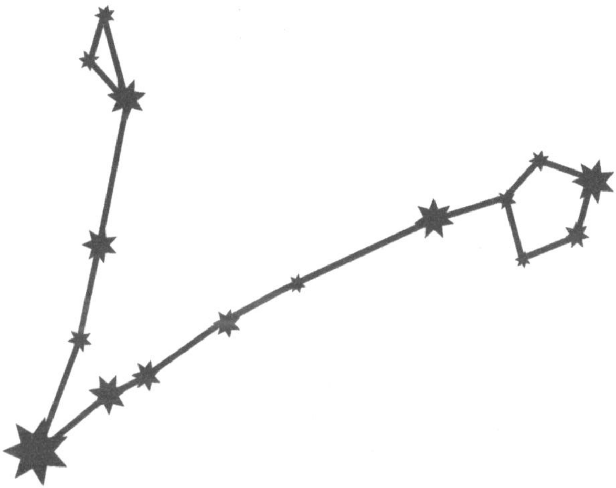

Published by Mango Publishing, a division of Mango Publishing Group, Inc.

For permission requests, please contact the publisher at:
Mango Publishing Group
5966 South Dixie Highway, Suite 300
Miami, FL 33143
info@mango.bz

For special orders, quantity sales, course adoptions and corporate sales, please email the publisher at sales@mango.bz. For trade and wholesale sales, please contact Ingram Publisher Services at customer.service@ingramcontent.com or +1.800.509.4887.

Paperback Edition: 978-1-68481-848-8

Printed in the United States of America

Pisces

a love letter

Heidi Rose Robbins

with illustrations by
Wyoh Lee

hello love.

(yes, you)

Friends,

I'm so glad you are holding this book! It is filled with encouragement and an ongoing invitation for us all to be more fully who we are.

The best way to work with these books is to purchase one for each of your signs — your Sun, Moon, and Rising Sign.

These are the three most important positions in your astrological chart. You can discover what these are if you enter your exact time, date, and place of birth in any online astrology site. Each position has something unique to offer.

When you read the book for your Moon, think of it as an energy that is very available to you. It's a place where you might feel comfortable. The Moon has to do with our emotional life, our patterns of behavior, and circumstances of our childhood. We can rely on the

Moon, but we also want to work to shed the patterns that no longer serve us.

The Sun is our present personality. We can learn a lot about our everyday self in the world. We can learn about the energies we have readily available to us to use in service to our highest calling.

The Rising Sign is the most important point. It is the sign that was rising as we took our first breath. It holds the key to our soul's calling. It is an energy we want to cultivate and be generous with throughout our lives.

So — enjoy the journey. Be sure to read
them all!

My dear Pisces,

This little book is a love letter to your compassionate and imaginative self. It is written to remind you of your many gifts. It is written to be a loving mirror so any page can remind you who you truly are. Take it in, dear Pisces. Breathe in the sensitivity and intuition that is YOU. See your all-embracing, redemptive self in these pages.

This little book will also explore those places in ourselves that start to close when we want to open, the part of us that hesitates when we want to act. We all have our quirks and difficulties, after all. But if we return again and again to our potency, vulnerability, and sense of possibility, we can outgrow our closures one by one.

Think of this book as a treasure chest containing the golden coins of YOU. Open it when you wish to remember your beauty, worth or great potential. And remember, too, this Pisces part of you is just one voice in the symphony of YOU. It cannot possibly contain your complexity and bounty. But it can begin to name just a few of your gifts.

Read this out loud when you can. Read this in the morning. Read it before bed. Read it when you need encouragement. Read it even if you are already feeling full of love and artistry. Let it fuel you. Own it and use it and claim it! This is your love letter, Pisces. This is the song of YOU.

Big love,
Heidi Rose

Celebrating Pisces

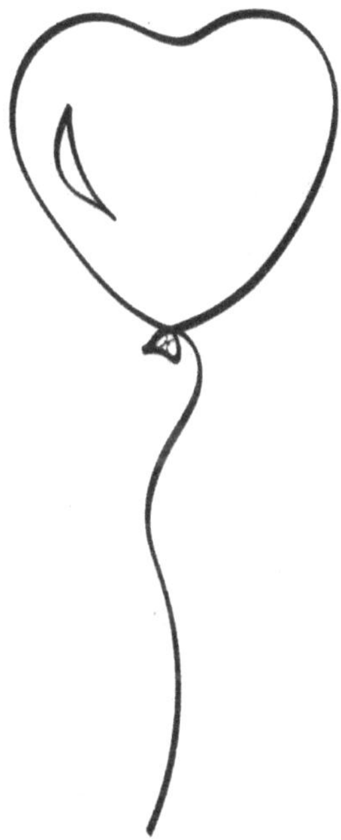

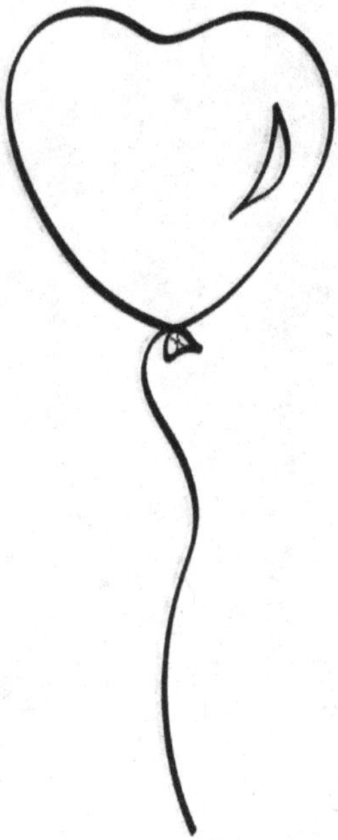

As you read this celebration, you will sometimes say "Yes, yes, yes! This is me!" And you may likewise sometimes feel that you have not yet lived into some of these qualities. This is honoring and celebrating the very best of your Pisces energy. This is naming the full, conscious, awakened use of your Pisces gifts. We are sounding the note of THE POSSIBLE. So, even if you feel you still have work to do in certain areas — as do we all — let these words be inspiration to offer your best Self!

Your sensitivity is vast.

You listen for what is between the lines, dear Pisces. You feel what is unspoken. Your empathy is strong. You detect and register all that is invisible. You take in and process all the undercurrents. You feel outward.

♓

You are a great lover of solitude.

You need a lot of alone time, dear Pisces. You need time with the sky and the sea and yourself. It takes a lot out of you to be 'out in the world.' You need time to turn off and recharge. Solitude also provides an opportunity to listen more deeply and you love that.

♓

Your offer your vast imagination through your artistry.

You love to dream, imagine, create, romanticize. You tell yourself stories, drift into other realms. You love to disappear into other worlds, delve into stories of adventure and love. Music and poetry inspire you and you offer up your own artistry when you are so inspired.

♓

You understand that we are all one.

You feel beneath the surface of our physical appearance. You know that we are all made of the same stuff. You understand that LOVE is the great connector and that at the root, we are all waves in one great ocean.

You work with ease behind the scenes.

You're the eye behind the camera, the power behind the throne, the one that makes it all happen behind the scenes. You move seamlessly behind the curtain, playing your part.

You are deeply intuitive.

You sense things. You know things before others do. You feel what needs to be said and how it might need to be said. You feel under and beneath the words we share.

♓

You shed tears for all of us.

Many people are unable to access their emotions in the way you are, dear Pisces. The depth of your feeling and the tears you shed allow us each to feel more deeply, to let compassion grow.

♓

You dream for us all.

You embody the "what-ifs." You carry hope. You paint a picture of the possible. You lovingly suggest a different outcome. You listen and connect us each with the divine. You let something greater pour through you, inspiring each of us.

You carry great depths within you.

Your quiet sometimes hides the vastness of you. You do not call attention to yourself. In fact, you do your best to avoid the spotlight, but those that sit with you are gifted with the depth of you. You require a certain intimacy and stillness to reveal the kingdoms (and queendoms) within.

♓

You are a great mystery.

You have a particular relationship with God or vastness or spaciousness or that which is greater than our individual selves. You have a relationship with all that is. You carry that. You also carry the mysteries of love and forgiveness. You might say, "It is better to live love than speak about it."

♓

You wash away what no longer serves.

Your sign is deeply connected with the ocean, dear Pisces. And the ocean erodes the old. It can also wash up and in one fell swoop eliminate what is no longer necessary. Much can be dissolved with love.

♓

You have the capacity to bring closure, end a pattern or finish a cycle.

Pluto is one of your rulers, dear Pisces. And Pluto rules death and rebirth. You understand the necessity of death, closure and completion. You can wrap things up or facilitate endings when so called.

You stand open and vulnerable, offering your compassion.

When you feel safe, your arms are open wide. You are a walking blessing or prayer. Your love goes out to many. You embrace those who most need your help. You do not ignore the needs of any along the way.

♓

You carry the seeds of redemption for us all.

You give everyone a second chance, dear Pisces. You believe in the possibility of a new cycle. You believe we should all be given the chance to begin again. You will always tend those that society ignores.

You are willing to listen and then listen more.

Your silence is inviting. Your eyes welcome intimacy. You listen when you are alone and you listen when you are with another. You are fully present. You receive. You hold what has been offered. And you return all you receive with love.

♓

You teach others about necessary solo replenishment.

You know the power of a good retreat. You know the power of time with oneself. You know you need it for yourself and when you give yourself that time, you inspire others to do the same.

♓

You teach us all about feeling connected to something greater than ourselves.

Pisces is all about our connection with the divine. You have your own unique connection with spaciousness and vastness and God, dear Pisces. You feel outward and know there is so very much more than this physical experience.

♓

You stand in and for love.

Pisces is the sign of unconditional love. You aspire to walk as love, dear Pisces. It's a lot. And of course, none of us fully succeed in such consistent embodiment. But you inspire us all to keep trying. Whatever is offered, you work to return in love.

Living Your Pisces Love

How are you feeling, dear Pisces? Can you sense the potency of your gifts? Do you want to make the very most of this loving energy of Pisces? Here are some thoughts about how to live fully into your Pisces love and how to nourish your Pisces spirit. Consider them little whispered reminders meant to help you THRIVE. Consider them 'action items'— a loving Pisces "to-do" list. Consider them invitations to live in the ocean of your sensitivity and care.

♓

Spend time near water.

Sit by a fountain, river, or lake. Walk along an ocean. Stand in the shower. Take a bath. Water is deeply nourishing for your spirit. It is as changeable and flowing as you are. It carries a kind of silence.

Write, paint or play music.

Let your artistry out to play.
Make time and space to create
and then let yourself go. Let your
love flow through all different
mediums. Sing. Move. Write poetry.
Let loose the beauty and bounty
of your imagination.

♓

Volunteer.

You feel everything and everyone. And you want to help. You will always feel relief when you choose an area where you can give of yourself. Work with the homeless, the hungry, those most in need.

Day dream.

When you give yourself time to dream, you touch the possible. You feel your connection with all that is. You open your mind far beyond the concrete concerns of the day and in so doing, you open to a greater connection with the subtler realms. When you are done dreaming, you share what you've touched with those you love.

♓

Consistently offer your compassion.

This is one of your great gifts. Never shy away from offering the love you feel. You are a great solace for many. You embody kindness for all those who are struggling.

♓

Have a spiritual practice.

You have a deep connection with the unseen worlds. You have an ability to stay open to the mystery, to the divine, to God. What is your spiritual path? Have one. It will bring great replenishment in your life.

♓

Spend Solo Time.

You give so much. You need to replenish. Take the time to completely unplug. Go on a solo retreat, or just close the door and spend an afternoon alone.

Growing Your Pisces Love

Sometimes, dear Pisces, we swing too far in one direction and need to invite a balancing energy to set us right. We are all growing and need to address the parts of ourselves that have not developed as fully. The opportunity for Pisces is to invite Virgo (your opposite sign) into the picture. Here are ways to grow your Pisces love to be practical, healthy and discerning about your most devoted work.

♓

Come out of hiding. Express.

It's easy to stay hidden when you're working behind the scenes. Don't be invisible. Make sure you are not letting shyness or uncertainty prevent the giving of your gifts.

♓

You can't save everyone.

Your heart goes out to so many. But you will completely deplete yourself without boundaries. Choose the areas where you know you can help. But also keep your own welfare and well-being in the equation.

♓

Address addiction.

Sometimes it all feels too much
and we want to escape.
Pisces rules addiction. Be careful
about the ways you choose to
release the pressure. The world
can feel harsh. Find the things
that will nourish and replenish you
and help you navigate
your sensitivity.

♓

Try to avoid the extremes of savior or victim.

Pisces is such a sign of extremes. We can be standing in unconditional love one moment and then feeling like the world and everyone in it is attacking us in another. Keep breathing in your own power and purpose. Don't collapse.

Be practical and grounded.

Try to avoid a sense of hopelessness or overwhelm. Take small steps. One small step will clarify and motivate. Don't give up. Tackle problems with breath and grounded action.

Work to address emotional problems with the power of the mind.

The light of the mind can help clarify or identify what feels overwhelming. See if you can name the pain and work practically to solve the problems. Use the power of the mind to avoid emotional overwhelm.

♓

Worrying won't help.

When we worry, we just compound the problem. We add fear to the issue at hand. Instead practice anticipating an ease-filled and graceful resolution. Bless the process. Don't chew on the worry bone.

♓

Practice ending what needs to end.

Pisces does rule endings, after all. Practice letting go, dear Pisces. Practice ending patterns that do not serve you. Bring in the power of Pluto to release what is no longer helpful so you can grow your love, light, and power.

Questions to Inspire Sharing Your Pisces Love

Dear Pisces, here are a few questions or prompts that might inspire or clarify your mission. Grab your journal. Write for 15 minutes about each. Read your answers out loud to a friend. Read them out loud for yourself. Let this exploration nourish your Pisces love and imagination.

What do I long for?

Write a poem in the next 3 minutes. Time yourself. Just dive in.

♓

What is my secret name?

♓

What is my greatest superpower?

♓

Here is a story about one of my childhood summers...

Here are 3 of my favorite songs and why I love them...

♓

Here is a story about
the ocean...

♓

My favorite body
of water is...
And this is why...

♓

When I am alone...

One Last Little Love Note:

Pisces, I hope those questions spark great love, artistry and dream-time in your life. You have so much to offer, so much to give. Your love and compassion inspire so many. If you ever need encouragement, just dip into this little book for a reminder of your light.

Now go forth Pisces, and do your thing.

The World is Waiting for YOU.

Big love,

Heidi Rose

About the Author.

Heidi grew up with an astrologer father and an architect mother. Her father taught her the zodiac with her ABC's and her mother taught her to love art and appreciate the beauty of the natural world. She likes to call herself a poet with a map of the heavens in her pocket. Her passion is to inspire and encourage us all to be our truest, most authentic, radiant selves using the tools of astrology and poetry.

www.heidirose.com

Instagram @heidiroserobbins

www.ingramcontent.com/pod-product-compliance
Lightning Source LLC
La Vergne TN
LVHW031212160826
845780LV00032B/299
* 9 7 8 1 6 8 4 8 1 8 4 8 8 *